# LAUGH
# —OUT—
# LOUD

POCKET

FOR BOYS

# LAUGH
## —OUT—
## LOUD
### POCKET

*Doodles*

## FOR BOYS

## ROB ELLIOTT

ILLUSTRATED BY JONNY HAWKINS

**Revell**

*a division of Baker Publishing Group*
Grand Rapids, Michigan

Text © 2015 by Rob Elliott
Illustrations © 2015 by Jonny Hawkins

Published by Revell
a division of Baker Publishing Group
P.O. Box 6287, Grand Rapids, MI 49516-6287
www.revellbooks.com

Printed in the United States of America

ISBN 978-0-8007-2236-4

15  16  17  18  19  20  21      7  6  5  4  3  2  1

# THE LAUGH-OUT-LOUD HUMOR CODE
### by Rob Elliott

1. Don't make jokes at other people's expense.

2. KEEP IT CLEAN.

3. LAUGHTER is Great Medicine, so find something to laugh at every day.

Rx
NOT To Be Taken Seriously

4. Tell your favorite jokes to as many people as you can to brighten up their days, too!

5. Body noise and Body fluid jokes are the best.

Toot!

# MY HUMOR CODE

1.

2.

3.

4.

5.

Write and doodle your own humor code.

# Q: WHAT HAPPENS WHEN RACE CAR DRIVERS EAT TOO MUCH?

A: THEY GET INDY-GESTION.

Doodle a driver stuffing his face and food flying by.

A: THEY DON'T LIKE BATS.

Doodle a big pitcher's head. What is in the cave?

# Q: WHY DIDN'T THE BOY TRUST THE OCEAN?

A: THERE WAS SOMETHING FISHY ABOUT IT.

Doodle what's fishy in and out
of the water. Add beach stuff too!

Q: WHERE DOES A SHIP GO WHEN IT'S NOT FEELING WELL?

A: TO SEE THE DOCK-TOR.

Draw who will help the sick ship.

# Q: WHAT DO YOU GET WHEN YOU HAVE BREAKFAST WITH A CENTIPEDE?

A: PANCAKES AND LEGS.

Doodle a stack of yummy pancakes. What's in them? Nuts? Chocolate chips? Earthworms?

Q: WHAT DO YOU CALL A DENTIST WHO CLEANS AN ALLIGATOR'S TEETH?

A: CRAZY!

Doodle a crazy dentist under a crazy dentist light.

## Q: WHY DID THE NINJA GO TO THE DOCTOR?

A: HE HAD KUNG FLU.

Fill in the ninja's face and doodle a goofy-looking doctor . . . with a nunchaku.

# Q: WHY WAS IT HOT IN THE STADIUM AFTER THE BASEBALL GAME?

A: ALL THE FANS LEFT.

Draw other overheated players. What's left in the stands? Cups? Popcorn? Keys?

# Q: WHAT DO YOU GET WHEN YOU CROSS AN ELEPHANT WITH DARTH VADER?

A: AN ELE-VADER.

Finish the crazy combination.

Q: WHAT IS A RACE CAR DRIVER'S
   FAVORITE MEAL?

A: FAST FOOD.

Can the driver make it to the finish line,
and can you finish doodling the joke?

Q: WHAT HAPPENED WHEN THE SPIDER
   GOT A NEW CAR?

A: IT TOOK IT FOR A SPIN.

Doodle a car around the spider.
Create cool web designs on it.

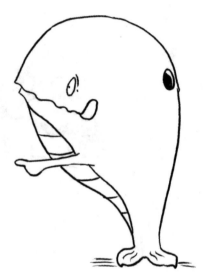

A: BLUBBER GUM.

Doodle his favorite candy and other fun and tasty stuff around him.

# Q: WHAT DO YOU CALL A BORING DINOSAUR?

A: A DINO-SNORE.

Hope you're not bored . . . because you
need to finish doodling this joke!

# Q: WHAT DO YOU GET WHEN AN ELEPHANT SNEEZES?

A: YOU GET OUT OF THE WAY!

Draw what is in the path of the sneeze. Grrrrrossss!

## Q: IF PEOPLE LIKE SANDWICHES, WHAT DO LIONS LIKE?

A: MAN-WICHES.

Doodle what's between the buns.

A: A NERVOUS REX.

Finish the dinosaur whose knees
are nervously knocking.

Q: WHAT DO YOU CALL A BOY WITH
   NO MONEY IN HIS POCKET?

A: NICKEL-LESS.

Doodle the rest of the boy
and his now out-of-pocket stuff.

KNOCK KNOCK.
  WHO'S THERE?
MINNOW.
  MINNOW WHO?
IF YOU CAN THINK OF A BETTER
  KNOCK-KNOCK JOKE, LET MINNOW.

Doodle what's holding up the minnow.
A fishbowl? Who's at the door?

Q: WHAT PLAYS MUSIC ON YOUR HEAD?

A: A HEADBAND.

Doodle music makers on the boy's head.

# Q: WHAT DOES A CLAM WEAR TO THE GYM?

A: A MUSSEL SHIRT.

Finish the clam near some weights.
Draw the mussel on his shirt.

KNOCK KNOCK.
  WHO'S THERE?
BACON.
  BACON WHO?
LET ME IN! I'M BACON OUT HERE!

Doodle the door, someone at the door, and a hot sun!

# Q: WHAT KIND OF PHOTOGRAPHS DO DENTISTS TAKE?

A: TOOTH PICS.

Whose teeth are these? Doodle the body
and the rest of the dentist too!

Q: WHAT KIND OF ANIMAL HAS THE BEST EYESIGHT?

A: A SEE LION.

We mustache you to connect the body to the tail!

Q: HOW DID THE BUNNY RABBIT FEEL
WHEN IT RAN OUT OF CARROTS?

A: VERY UNHOPPY.

Doodle the rabbit stopping, not
hopping. Hide some carrots.

**Q: WHY ARE CHICKENS SO BAD AT BASEBALL?**

A: BECAUSE THEY'RE ALWAYS HITTING FOWL BALLS.

Who struck the clucker? Doodle
other fine feathered players.

Q: WHAT DO MAGICIANS LIKE TO EAT FOR BREAKFAST?

A: TRIX CEREAL.

Finish the magician. Make his absence disappear.

Q: WHERE DO MONKEYS MAKE THEIR BURGERS?

A: ON THE GRILL-A.

Finish the griller!

Q: WHAT KIND OF ANIMAL WILL NEVER LEAVE YOU ALONE?

A: A BADGER.

Finish the badger.

## Q: WHAT DO CARS AND ELEPHANTS HAVE IN COMMON?

A: THEY BOTH HAVE TRUNKS.

Doodle a car atop the elephant . . . with its trunk open!

KNOCK KNOCK.
  WHO'S THERE?
ROBIN.
  ROBIN WHO?
NO, ROBIN HOOD. HE STEALS FROM
  THE RICH AND GIVES TO THE POOR.

Finish Robin, the door, and the answerer.

# Q: WHAT DOES A MOOSE LIKE TO PLAY AT PARTIES?

A: MOOSE-ICAL CHAIRS.

Doodle a rival moose horning in on his chair.

Q: WHEN DO YOU KNOW A TIGER ISN'T TELLING THE TRUTH?

A: WHEN IT'S A LION.

Doodle a big hat for this big cat.

Q: WHO LEADS THE ORCHESTRA AT THE ZOO?

A: THE BOA CONDUCTOR.

Finish the snake. What's he squeezing?
Is it an instrument?

Q: WHAT KIND OF CAR DOES A DEEP-
   SEA DIVER DRIVE?

A: A SCUBARU.

Finish the car and doodle some more deep-sea life.

## Q: WHAT KIND OF BUGS LIKE TO SNEAK UP ON YOU?

A: SPY-DERS.

Who's he watching? Finish the object he's behind.

Q: WHAT DOES A LEOPARD SAY AFTER HE EATS HIS DINNER?

A: "THAT HIT THE SPOT!"

Finish the table. Who's eating with him?

Q: WHY DID THE PLANT GO TO THE
   DENTIST?

A: IT NEEDED A ROOT CANAL.

Doodle the dentist and his toothy tools.

Q: WHAT KIND OF DOGS CHOP DOWN TREES?

A: LUMBER JACK RUSSELLS.

Finish the falling tree. Make the bark fly.

Q: WHAT IS A GOLFER'S FAVORITE DRINK?

A: ICED TEE.

Finish the golfer with club in hand.

## Q: WHAT IS A FRISBEE'S FAVORITE KIND OF MUSIC?

A: DISK-O.

Who's dancing?

A: ELK-ASELTZER.

Finish the poor, ailing deer!

# Q: WHAT KIND OF CLOTHES DO DISOBEDIENT CHILDREN WEAR?

A: THEY WEAR SMARTY-PANTS.

Finish his clothing.
What about his sis? Doodle her.

Q: WHAT HAPPENED AFTER THE MAN ACCIDENTLY DROPPED HIS COFFEE IN THE VOLCANO?

A: JAVA CAME OUT!

Where's the man holding his fresh-brewed coffee from fresh grounds?

Q: WHERE DOES THE HORSE GO WHEN HE'S SICK?

A: THE HORSE-PITAL.

Doodle the medical building. Is there a mare nurse in the window?

# Q: WHY WAS THE SKELETON LAUGHING?

A: BECAUSE HE FOUND HIS HUMERUS.

Can you find his humerus? Label all his bones
. . . hee-hee. Draw his bony son too.

Q: HOW DID THE BARBER WIN
THE RACE?

A: HE TOOK A SHORTCUT.

Who is the barber racing and chasing?

Q: WHAT DO YOU GET WHEN YOU
BORROW MONEY FROM A BISON?

A: A BUFFA-LOAN.

Who is the borrower asking for buffalo
nickels and dimes and dollars?

Q: WHAT DOES A WEASEL LIKE TO READ?

A: POP-UP BOOKS.

What's up? That is, what's popping up from the book?

# Q: HOW DID THE MARCHING BAND KEEP THEIR TEETH CLEAN?

A: WITH A TUBA TOOTHPASTE.

Where is the toothpaste? Could it be on another marcher?

Q: HOW DO COMEDIANS LIKE THEIR EGGS?

A: FUNNY-SIDE UP.

Draw a funny guy next to her. Maybe it's *you!*

Q: WHY WOULDN'T THE LIONS PLAY GAMES WITH THE ZEBRAS?

A: THERE WERE TOO MANY CHEETAHS.

Where are those cheetahs?

# Q: HOW DOES JACK FROST GET AROUND?

A: ON HIS MOTOR-ICICLE.

Draw Jack's freezing wheels beneath
him. Vroom, vroom!

Q: WHAT DO YOU GET WHEN YOU CROSS
A BEAR WITH A PIG?

A: A GRIZZLY BOAR.

Draw the wacky combo in between these two.

Q: WHY DID THE POLICEMAN GO TO THE BASEBALL GAME?

A: HE HEARD SOMEONE HAD STOLEN SECOND BASE.

Draw a ball field . . . and some players . . . and a base!

# Q: WHAT IS A TREE'S FAVORITE DRINK?

A: ROOT BEER.

Draw a big mug of this bubbly soda!

Q: WHAT DO YOU CALL A SLEEPING BULL?

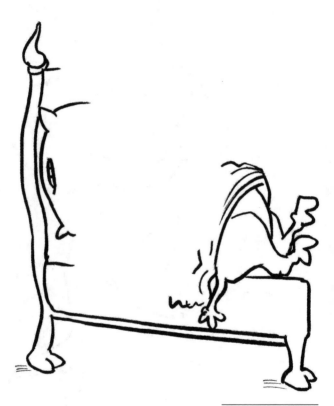

A: A BULLDOZER.

You snooze, you lose. Draw the snoring beast!

# Q: WHAT DO BUMBLEBEES PLAY AT THE PARK?

A: FRIS-BEE.

What buzzing buddy threw the disc?

# Q: WHERE DO DUCKS LIVE IN THE CITY?

A: IN THEIR POND-OMINIUMS.

Doodle a duck dynasty with buildings and
such. And draw a nice big pond below.

A: THE TEACHER SAID IT WOULD BE A PIECE OF CAKE.

Fill in the thought balloon and doodle the joke!

# Q: WHERE DOES THE CATCHER SIT WHEN IT'S TIME FOR DINNER?

A: BEHIND THE PLATE.

Finish the catcher and have him devouring some food.

Q: WHY DID THE SNAKE CROSS
   THE ROAD?

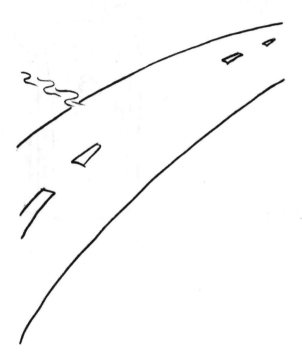

A: TO GET TO THE OTHER SSSSSSSIDE.

Where's the snake? Other critters?

Q: WHY WOULDN'T ANYONE LAUGH AT THE TOWEL'S JOKES?

A: BECAUSE IT HAD A DRY SENSE OF HUMOR.

Rack up an audience. Or is he telling jokes to the scale? A sponge? Soap?

# Q: WHY CAN'T YOU TRUST AN ARTIST?

A: BECAUSE THEY'RE SKETCHY.

What's so sketchy? Sketch it!

# Q: WHO TOOK THE OCTOPUS?

A: THE SQUIDNAPPER.

Ink the squidnapper!

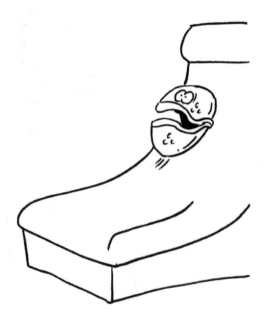

Q: WHAT DID THE ALMOND SAY TO THE PSYCHIATRIST?

A: "EVERYBODY SAYS I'M NUTS!"

Where's the psychiatrist? What's the rest of his office look like?

# Q: WHAT DO YOU GET WHEN YOU PLAY BASKETBALL IN HAWAII?

A: HULA-HOOPS!

Draw a grass-skirted player and a shark shooter!

Q: WHAT DO YOU GET WHEN YOU THROW NOODLES IN A JACUZZI?

A: SPA-GHETTI.

Finish the meatball. Who's throwing it in?
Draw the relaxed pasta in their jacuzzi!

# Q: WHAT IS THE MOST COLORFUL SNAKE IN THE WORLD?

A: A RAIN-BOA CONSTRICTOR.

Add lines (and color them if you can) to the snake.
What in the foreground will be his main squeeze?

Q: WHAT KIND OF TREE NEEDS
A DOCTOR ALL THE TIME?

A: A SYCAMORE TREE.

Draw the doc who can help this poor old sap.

Q: WHAT IS THE BEST TIME TO VISIT THE DENTIST?

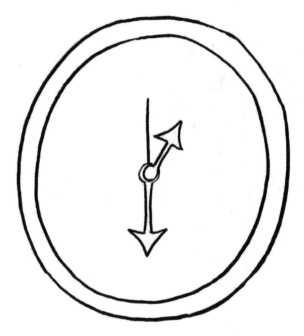

A: AT TOOTH-THIRTY.

Draw the number of teeth on the face of the clock where the numerals go. Doodle the rest of the joke.

A: A SWALLOW.

Where is the birdie? What's on the plate? On the fork?

Q: WHAT DOES A BLACK BELT EAT FOR LUNCH?

A: KUNG-FOOD!

Be a martial artist and draw the boy wearing the black belt. Other karate chopping food?

Q: WHAT DOES A COW KEEP IN ITS WALLET?

A: A WHOLE LOT OF MOO-LA.

Fill this cash cow with happy coins and dollars and other milk money.

Q: WHAT DID THE BOY SAY WHEN HE THREW A SLUG ACROSS THE ROOM?

A: "MY, HOW SLIME FLIES!"

Doodle the slug-throwing boy and more slime!

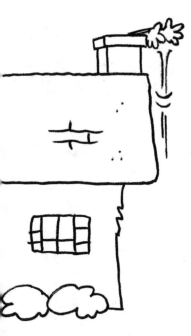

A: SQUASH.

Draw the resulting effect of the dropped pumpkin.

Q: WHY DID THE CHEF HAVE TO STOP COOKING?

A: HE RAN OUT OF THYME.

What's on the chef's spice rack? What about herbs?

A: IN A CROCK-POT!

What's in the pot? Is it hot?

# Q: WHY IS THE OCEAN SO MUCH FUN?

A: YOU CAN ALWAYS HAVE A WHALE OF A TIME.

Doodle other sea creatures leaping
and laughing over the whale.

**Q: WHAT DO YOU DO WHEN YOU COME UPON TWO SNAILS FIGHTING?**

**A: LET THEM SLUG IT OUT.**

Come out of your shell and draw
the other fighting slug!

# Q: WHAT SOMETIMES RUNS BUT NEVER WALKS?

A: YOUR NOSE.

Make his nose run! What's getting away
from the running nose (yuck!)?

Q: WHY DID THE BOY STOP USING HIS PENCIL?

A: IT WAS POINTLESS.

Get the lead out and finish the pencil.
What was it drawing? What broke it?

# Q: WHAT HAS FOUR WHEELS AND FLIES?

A: A GARBAGE TRUCK.

Who's driving? Don't refuse to decorate the truck!

Q: WHY DID THE FROG GET SENT HOME FROM SCHOOL?

A: HE WAS A BULLY-FROG!

Draw the head and face of this unhoppy meanie!

Q: WHERE DOES A BEAVER KEEP
   ITS MONEY?

A: IN THE RIVER BANK.

Draw the joke and some floating cash.

# Q: WHAT DO YOU GET WHEN YOU CROSS A VULTURE WITH A BUMBLEBEE?

A: A BU22-ARD.

Doodle this hilarious and hideous creature!

# Q: WHAT'S A WOLF'S FAVORITE TREAT?

A: PIGS IN A BLANKET.

Draw the rest of these squeal meals.

Q: WHAT'S A BIRD'S FAVORITE MOVIE?

A: BATMAN AND ROBIN.

Let 'er fly! Doodle it!

Q: WHY DID THE HOUSE GO TO THE
DOCTOR?

A: IT HAD A LOT OF WINDOWPANES.

Draw the windowpanes and other accessories.

A: IN CASE THERE WAS ANY CHANGE IN THE WEATHER.

Doodle a coin storm out of a cloud bank.

Q: WHY WAS THE MATH TEACHER SAD?

A: HE HAD A LOT OF PROBLEMS TO SOLVE.

What's on the board that makes him so sad?

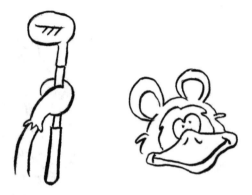

Finish the monkey. Add his bag of clubs,
a golf ball, and background.

# Q: WHEN DOES THE KING HAVE TROUBLE BREATHING?

A: WHEN HE DOESN'T HAVE ANY HEIR.

Draw who isn't his heir who is there.

Q: WHY DID THE BEAR EAT A LAMP?

A: IT JUST WANTED A LIGHT SNACK.

Draw the rest of the bear chomping down the furniture.

Q: WHY WERE ALL THE ANIMALS
   LAUGHING AT THE OWL?

A: BECAUSE HE WAS A HOOT.

Doodle other wildlife having a wild laugh.

Q: WHAT'S A GOOD THING TO EAT WHEN YOU'RE FEELING STRESSED?

A: A MARSH-MELLOW.

Draw a campfire and the other mellow fellow.

Q: WHY DID THE PEOPLE PUCKER UP EVERY TIME THEY DROVE AROUND TOWN?

A: BECAUSE THEY WERE DRIVING A LEMON.

Doodle a car that looks like a lemon.

Q: WHY DID THE REPORTER GO TO THE ICE CREAM PARLOR?

A: HE WANTED TO GET THE SCOOP!

Who's holding the scooper . . . and being interviewed?

Q: HOW DID THE TUBA CALL THE
   TRUMPET?

A: ON HIS SAXO-PHONE.

Draw the trumpet . . . and the joke.

Q: WHERE DO SHARKS GO ON
   SATURDAY NIGHTS?

A: TO THE DIVE-IN MOVIES.

Doodle the movie he's chomping at the bit to see.

# Q: WHY ARE THERE FROGS ON THE BASEBALL TEAM?

A: TO CATCH THE FLY BALLS.

Finish froggy and add a homerun fence.

Q: WHY DIDN'T THE BOY WANT TO GO CAMPING OVER THE WEEKEND?

A: IT WAS TOO IN-TENTS FOR HIM!

What are in the tents?

Q: HOW CAN YOU LEARN MORE ABOUT
   SPIDERS?

A: CHECK OUT THEIR WEB-SITE.

Doodle his website. What does it spell or catch?

Q: WHY DID THE METEOR GO TO HOLLYWOOD?

A: IT WANTED TO BE A STAR.

Doodle the famous "Hollywood" sign on the
mountain and put stars in the skies.

Q: WHAT DO YOU GET WHEN YOU CROSS A SNOWMAN WITH A LION?

A: FROSTBITE!

Doodle a snowy lion's head with its mouth wide open.

# Q: WHAT IS THE TASTIEST PLACE TO LAND IF YOU SHIPWRECK?

A: A DESSERT ISLAND.

Doodle delicious delights.

Q: WHAT KIND OF VEGETABLE IS LAZY AND IRRESPONSIBLE?

A: A DEAD-BEET.

Doodle a remote in the hands
of a couch potato next to him.

Q: WHAT'S THE BEST WAY TO PLAY A SCARY VIDEO GAME?

A: ON A BIG-SCREAM TV.

What's on the screaming big screen?

Q: WHAT DO YOU CALL A REPTILE THAT STARTS FIGHTS?

A: AN INSTA-GATOR.

Who's wrestling the gator?

Q: WHAT DID THE TREE SAY
   TO THE FLOWER?

A: "I'M ROOTING FOR YOU."

Doodle a big, beautiful tree talking to its bud.

Q: WHAT DID THE MOTHER POSSUM
   SAY TO HER SON?

A: "QUIT HANGING AROUND ALL DAY
        AND DO SOMETHING!"

Doodle the son. What's below them?

KNOCK KNOCK.
  WHO'S THERE?
RADIO.
  RADIO WHO?
"RADIO OR NOT, HERE I COME!"

Doodle a television answering the
door. Where's the remote?

KNOCK KNOCK.
  WHO'S THERE?
CONNOR.
  CONNOR WHO?
CONNOR BROTHER COME OUT
  AND PLAY?

Who's the knocker?

Q: WHAT DID THE PEN SAY TO THE PENCIL?

A: "YOU'RE LOOKING SHARP TODAY!"

Pick up a pencil and draw a pen. What's pencil's reply?

# Q: WHAT DO YOU CALL A FISH WITH NO EYES?

A: FSH.

Doodle the rest of the fish with no eyes.
Where is its seeing-eye dogfish?

KNOCK KNOCK.
  WHO'S THERE?
CARRIE.
  CARRIE WHO?
CARRIE MY BOOKS FOR ME?

Finish the book-carrying one. Doodle the
door and the dude being asked.

Q: WHAT DOES A CAT WEAR AT NIGHT?

A: ITS PAW-JAMAS.

Complete the cat in its nightclothes.

Q: WHAT DO YOU GIVE A MOUSE
ON HIS BIRTHDAY?

A: CHEESECAKE.

Doodle the rest of the cake with candles. Finish
the table and draw friends and balloons.

FRED: TODAY THE TEACHER WAS
    YELLING AT ME FOR SOMETHING
    I DIDN'T DO!
MOM: WHAT WAS THAT?
FRED: MY HOMEWORK.

Doodle Mom looking surprised!

Q: WHAT KIND OF DOG CRIES
   THE MOST?

A: CHI-WAH-WAH!

Finish the bawling little dog and draw its pal.

# Q: WHAT DO YOU GET WHEN YOU CROSS A PIG WITH A CHRISTMAS TREE?

A: A PORK-U-PINE.

Finish this wacky combo and decorate it.

Q: NAME TWO DAYS OF THE WEEK THAT START WITH T.

A: "TODAY" AND "TOMORROW."

Fill in a funny calendar. Make up some crazy days.

# Q: WHAT DO YOU CALL A STICK THAT WON'T DO ANYTHING YOU WANT?

A: A STICK-IN-THE-MUD.

Doodle the stick that is stuck. What's its friend saying?

# Q: WHAT ARE THE FUNNIEST FISH AT THE AQUARIUM?

A: CLOWN FISH.

Finish the funny fish. Is there a clown school of fish?

Q: WHY DID THE CREDIT CARD
   GO TO JAIL?

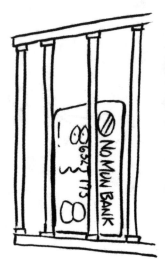

A: IT WAS GUILTY AS CHARGED!

Who's visiting? Cash? Check? Money order?

# Q: WHAT DO YOU HAVE IF YOUR DOG CAN'T BARK?

A: A HUSHPUPPY.

Doodle a doggy who can't make a sound.
Where is its loudly dressed owner?

# Q: WHY CAN'T YOU TRUST A PIG?

A: IT WILL ALWAYS SQUEAL ON YOU.

Give the pig some expression.

# Q: WHAT FRUIT TEASES PEOPLE A LOT?

A: A BA-NA-NA-NA-NA-NA-NA!

Doodle the fruit being teased. Bad banana!

A: BECAUSE HE WAS A RULER.

Finish the royal smallish one.

Q: WHY WAS THE INCREDIBLE HULK SO GOOD AT GARDENING?

A: HE HAD A GREEN THUMB.

Doodle Hulk's head with a flower in his teeth.

Q: WHAT DID THE ROBBER SAY WHEN HE STOLE FROM THE BOOKSTORE?

A: "I'D BETTER BOOK IT ON OUT OF HERE!"

Finish the thief's head. Who's chasing him? Draw a bookstore door.

Q: WHAT DID THE POOL SAY
   TO THE LAKE?

A: "WATER YOU DOING HERE?"

Where is the lake? Water you waiting for? Doodle it!

# Q: WHEN DOES THE ROAD GET ANGRY?

A: WHEN SOMEONE CROSSES IT.

Who crossed it . . . or who's waiting to cross it?

KNOCK KNOCK.
  WHO'S THERE?
RABBIT.
  RABBIT WHO?
RABBIT CAREFULLY. IT'S A CHRISTMAS
  PRESENT.

Finish rabbit carefully.

A: HE WAS BRAINSTORMING.

Doodle lightning striking his head and a thought balloon raining. Draw strange inventions he's made.

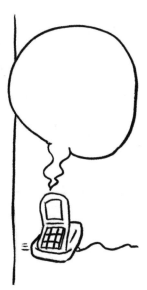

A: IT WILL LEAVE A DETAILED MOOSE-AGE.

Doodle a moose's message. Doodle
a calling moose on the left.

Q: WHY DID THE COWBOY ASK HIS
   CATTLE SO MANY QUESTIONS?

A: BECAUSE HE WANTED TO GRILL THEM.

Doodle a cowboy next to his grill waving
a spatula. What's he asking?

Q: WHERE DOES A LIZARD KEEP
   HIS GROCERIES?

A: IN THE REFRIGER-GATOR.

Doodle another lizard with a stack of cool items.

A: IN A GRAVY BOAT.

Finish turkey's head and anything else that meats your eye.

Q: WHAT DID THE WOLF DO WHEN HE HEARD THE JOKE?

A: HE HOWLED.

Doodle a big smiling moon and stars.

**Q: WHAT DID THE SPIDER SAY TO THE FLY?**

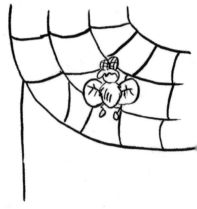

A: "WHY DON'T YOU STICK AROUND FOR A WHILE?"

Doodle a hungry spider hanging on by a thread.

Q: WHAT DO YOU GET WHEN YOU CROSS A COW WITH A TOAD?

A: A BULLFROG.

Doodle this combo cow/frog. Now, hop to it!

# Q: WHAT HAPPENED WHEN THE TURKEY GOT IN A FIGHT?

A: HE GOT THE STUFFING KNOCKED OUT OF HIM.

Who's he fighting? Where's the stuffing?

Q: WHAT PERFORMS AT THE CIRCUS AND FLIES AROUND EATING MOSQUITOS?

A: AN ACRO-BAT.

Finish the bat's wings . . . and head . . . and skeeter needs a face too.

Q: HOW DO YOU SNEAK ACROSS THE DESERT WITHOUT BEING SEEN?

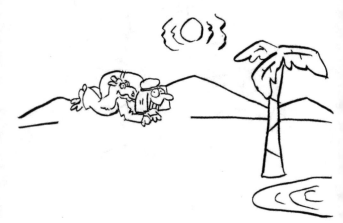

A: YOU WEAR CAMEL-FLAGE.

Doodle a camel beneath Mr. Sneaky.

# TONGUE TWISTER:
## SAY IT 10 TIMES FAST . . .
## TICKLING TINY TURKEY TOES.

Doodle a hysterically laughing
gobbler with feathers flying!

Q: WHY DID THE MOOSE WORK OUT
   AT THE GYM?

A: BECAUSE HE WANTED BIG MOOSE-LES.

Doodle moose's growing arms as they lift
tree limb weights . . . or dumbbells.

Q: WHY DID THE CHEETAH
   GET GLASSES?

A: BECAUSE IT WAS SEEING SPOTS.

Do a spot drawing of his head . . .
and don't forget the glasses!

Q: WHAT IS THE RICHEST BIRD
IN THE WORLD?

A: THE GOLDEN EAGLE.

Be regal and finish the wealthy eagle.

Q: WHERE DOES A VOLCANO WASH ITS HANDS?

A: IN THE LAVA-TORY.

Doodle the joke.

Q: WHAT DO DINOSAURS PUT IN THEIR CARS?

A: FOSSIL FUEL.

Where's dino's dome? Doodle it.
Face it—he needs one.

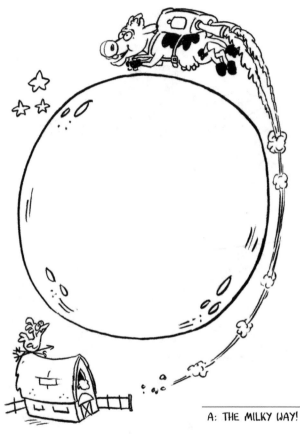

Q: WHICH WAY DID THE COW JUMP OVER THE MOON?

A: THE MILKY WAY!

What's on the moooon?

A: A ROW BOT.

What other tech toys might spring out of the water?

Q: WHAT DO YOU CALL A COW WHO CAN'T GIVE MILK?

A: A MILK DUD.

Where is the dairy farmer? Is he sad?
Where are the chickens?

Q: HOW DID THE OYSTER GET TO THE HOSPITAL?

A: IN A CLAM-BULANCE.

Design its side. Who's driving? Other traffic?

# Q: WHY WAS THE SNAKE SO FUNNY?

A: HIS JOKES WERE HISS-TERICAL.

Give snake some fun and funny drawings.
Who is snake's audience?

A: THE BEETLES.

Finish bug. Have him dancing. Where are his CDs?

A: FERRY TALES.

Design the book cover and add a ferry in the background.

# Q: WHAT DOES A MONSTER PUT ON HIS HOT FUDGE SUNDAE?

A: WHIPPED SCREAM.

Doodle the rest of his sundae.
Add toppings! Scary good!

KNOCK KNOCK.
  WHO'S THERE?
PAWS.
  PAWS WHO?
CAN YOU PAWS FOR A MOMENT AND
  OPEN THE DOOR?

Whose two paws are those? Finish
doodling the door too!

Q: WHAT DO PEANUT BUTTER AND
   JELLY DO AROUND THE CAMPFIRE?

A: THEY TELL TOAST STORIES.

Where's jelly? Draw a tent in the back.

Q: WHY COULDN'T THE MONSTER
GO TO SLEEP?

A: HE WAS AFRAID THERE WERE CHILDREN UNDER HIS BED.

Finish the monster's bed. Are there kids
under there? Where's Dad and Mom?

KNOCK KNOCK.
  WHO'S THERE?
ACHOO.
  ACHOO WHO?
ACHOO MY GUM EVERY DAY!

Who's chewing and blowing the bubble?
Finish doodling him. Who's at the door?

Q: WHAT DO COWBOYS LIKE ON THEIR SALADS?

A: RANCH DRESSING.

Build a big horse salad with ranch dressing.

A: CHOCO-LATE.

Where is candy going? Confection convention? Suh-weeeet!

Q: WHAT DO YOU GET WHEN YOU CROSS A MONKEY WITH A PEACH?

A: AN APE-RICOT.

Finish the fruit-faced beast. Don't forget his dragging arms.

# Q: WHERE DO BEES COME FROM?

A: STING-APORE AND BEE-LIVIA.

Doodle the bee's head and antennae and wings.
Write on his suitcase where he's been.

Q: WHAT DO YOU CALL A PIG THAT'S
   NO FUN TO BE AROUND?

A: A BOAR.

Finish this dull and angry pig.

Q: WHERE CAN YOU GO TO SEE MUMMIES OF COWS?

A: THE MOO-SEUM OF NATURAL HISTORY.

Can you mooove your pen and draw another cow mummy?

# Q: WHAT DO YOU DO IF YOUR DOG STEALS YOUR SPELLING HOMEWORK?

A: YOU TAKE THE WORDS RIGHT OUT OF HIS MOUTH!

Doodle the homework-happy hound tugging back.

**Q: HOW COME HYENAS ARE SO HEALTHY?**

**A: BECAUSE LAUGHTER IS THE BEST MEDICINE.**

Finish hyena and draw a treadmill under him.

Q: WHAT IS AS BIG AS AN ELEPHANT BUT WEIGHS ZERO POUNDS?

A: AN ELEPHANT'S SHADOW.

Doodle the elephant's shadow.

# Q: HOW DO YOU GREET A TOAD?

A: "WART'S UP?"

Doodle a friendly toad. What is it saying?

Q: WHAT DOES A SQUIRREL LIKE
TO EAT FOR BREAKFAST?

A: DOUGH-NUTS.

Finish squirrel. Don't forget his bushy
tail (with doughnuts hidden in it).

## Q: WHAT'S THE DIFFERENCE BETWEEN A CAT AND A FROG?

A: A CAT HAS NINE LIVES AND A FROG CROAKS EVERY DAY!

Finish the friends and their funny faces.

Q: WHAT DID THE ELEVATOR SAY TO ITS FRIEND?

A: "I THINK I'M COMING DOWN WITH SOMETHING."

Who's the friend? Stairs? Step?
Spiral staircase? Rope?

Q: WHY WAS THE SCIENCE TEACHER ANGRY?

A: HE WAS A MAD SCIENTIST.

Doodle his mad head with wacky hair and big glasses.

Q: WHAT DO BIRDS DO BEFORE THEY WORK OUT?

A: THEIR WORM-UPS.

Use your bird brain and finish the bird's head.
Don't forget his target . . . the worms.

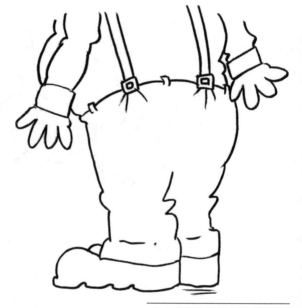

A: WITH A CABBAGE PATCH.

Draw the joke on farmer's breeches.

A: FINDING HALF A WORM IN YOUR APPLE!

Wiggle your pencil onto your page
and squiggle the joke.

CUSTOMER: EXCUSE ME, WAITER, BUT IS THERE SPAGHETTI ON THE MENU?
WAITER: NO, BUT I BELIEVE WE HAVE SOME IN THE KITCHEN.

Use your noodle and doodle the spaghetti. What else is in it?

Q: WHY WAS EVERYONE LOOKING UP AT THE CEILING AND CHEERING?

A: THEY WERE CEILING FANS.

Doodle a decorative fan and add a person (or animal) cheering between these two.

Q: WHAT DO TREES EAT FOR BREAKFAST?

A: OAKMEAL.

Doodle the top of the tree and what it's eating.

Q: WHAT DID ONE TUBE OF GLUE SAY TO THE OTHER?

A: "LET'S STICK TOGETHER!"

Where is the other tube? Stick to it and doodle it!

## Q: WHAT HAPPENS WHEN YOU PHONE A CLOWN THREE TIMES?

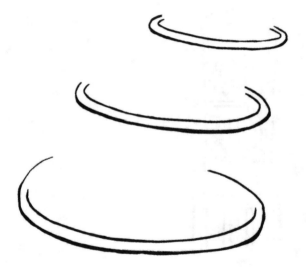

A: A THREE-RING CIRCUS.

Fill the three rings with circus performers.

# Q: WHAT GETS WET WHILE IT DRIES?

A: A TOWEL.

What used the towel? Your face? Your dog? Your cat?

Q: HOW CAN YOU KEEP SOMEONE IN SUSPENSE?

A: I'LL TELL YOU LATER.

Who is asking the question?

A: A CAT-ASTROPHE.

Finish the lion. Where are the bent cage bars?

A: KNEECAPS.

Doodle the joke. I'm not pulling your leg.

Q: WHAT'S THE BEST KIND OF DOG
   TO SHOOT HOOPS WITH?

A: A BASKET HOUND.

Doodle a dribbling, driving, dunking doggy!

Q: WHAT IS A ZUCCHINI'S FAVORITE GAME?

A: SQUASH.

Who is zucchini serving? Use your gourd and draw the court too.

KNOCK KNOCK.
  WHO'S THERE?
KETCHUP.
  KETCHUP WHO?
LET ME COME IN SO WE CAN KETCHUP.

Doodle a door and a hot dog behind it.

# Q: WHAT DID THE ALIEN SAY TO THE FLOWER BED?

A: "TAKE ME TO YOUR WEEDER."

Doodle an out-of-this-world alien with strange antennae and hands for feet.

KNOCK KNOCK.
  WHO'S THERE?
SHERWOOD.
  SHERWOOD WHO?
SHERWOOD ENJOY COMING IN AND
  SEEING YOU!

Doodle his best buddy on the other side of the door.

KNOCK KNOCK.
WHO'S THERE.
FUNNEL.
  FUNNEL WHO?
THE FUNNEL START WHEN I COME IN.

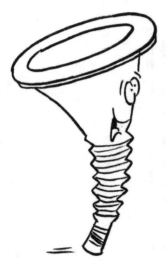

Doodle a door . . . and one who's
behind it that's bored.

Q: HOW DID THE BASEBALL PLAYER
   LOSE HIS HOUSE?

A: HE MADE HIS HOME RUN.

Feel at home doodling the boy's running house.

A: DADDY LONG LEGOS.

Doodle a building block body and head.

Q: HOW DO SKUNKS GET IN TOUCH WITH EACH OTHER?

A: THEY USE THEIR SMELL PHONES.

To whom is skunk sending this smellfie?

Q: WHAT DID THE BIRD WEAR
   TO THE BALL?

A: A DUCKS-EDO.

Finish the bird's ball suit.

KNOCK KNOCK.
  WHO'S THERE?
LENA.
  LENA WHO?
LENA LITTLE CLOSER AND I'LL TELL
  YOU ANOTHER JOKE.

Who's telling the joke? Lean over and doodle it!

A: ROADKILL.

Doodle an oncoming roadster.

Q: WHAT KIND OF BUGS WEAR
   SNEAKERS?

A: SHOE FLIES.

Doodle the joke!

KNOCK KNOCK.
  WHO'S THERE?
EDDY.
  EDDY WHO?
EDDY-BODY HOME?

Finish Eddy's body.

Q: WHAT DO YOU GET WHEN A CAT CLIMBS DOWN YOUR CHIMNEY WITH A BAG OF PRESENTS?

A: SANTA PAWS.

Draw on the bag what's in the bag.

A: DUCK, DUCK, GOOSE.

Doodle others players, like a duck and a goose.

JOE: DID THAT DOLPHIN SPLASH YOU ON ACCIDENT?
BILL: NO, IT WAS ON PORPOISE!

Doodle Bill being splashed.

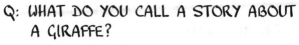

Q: WHAT DO YOU CALL A STORY ABOUT A GIRAFFE?

A: A TALL TALE.

Finish the giraffe and the title.

Q: WHERE DO DOGS GO IF THEY LOSE THEIR TAILS?

A: THE RETAIL STORE.

Doodle a store behind the dog.

Q: HOW CAN YOU TELL IF A MOOSE HAS BEEN IN YOUR FREEZER?

A: BY THE MOOSE TRACKS.

Finish doodling the joke.

No joke! Draw yourself telling your favorite
joke. Who's in the audience?

Doodle yourself telling a great barnyard joke. Add a horse and pig . . . and make them a laughingstock.

## Q: WHERE DOES A SUPERHERO VACATION?

A: ANYWHERE THAT STARTS WITH "THE CAPE."

Finish this superhero and write your own
super joke beneath it. Starring you?

Q: WHAT SHIRT IS ONLY WORN ON TUESDAYS AND THURSDAYS?

A: A T-SHIRT.

Design a shirt that fits you to a tee.

Q: WHAT TWO WORDS MAKE IT SOUND
   LIKE A QUARTERBACK WANTS
   TO GO HOME?

A: "HUT HUT!"

Doodle the center who snaps the ball
and the players around him.

KNOCK KNOCK.
   WHO'S THERE?
WEIRDO.
   WEIRDO WHO?
WEIRDO YOU THINK YOU'RE GOING?

Doodle a door and a frightened friend behind it.

# Q: WHAT'S A PICKLE'S FAVORITE INSTRUMENT?

A: A CUKE-ELELE.

Doodle the little instrument
he's a-picklin' and a-grinnin'.

Q: WHAT DO YOU CALL A PIG
   ON WHEELS?

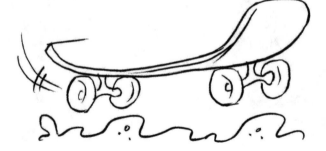

A: A SKATE-BOAR.

Use your pen and oink and doodle a fantastic pig!

Q: WHAT DOES A BARBER CALL
HIS FLYING MACHINE?

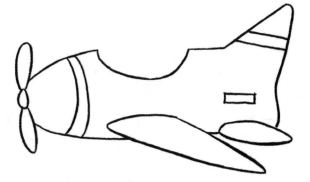

A: A HAIRPLANE!

Doodle a barber or a long-haired
pilot who needs a haircut.

Q: WHAT IS A MONSTER'S FAVORITE PASTA DISH?

A: GHOUL-ASH!

Doodle it!

Q: WHEN CAN YOU WALK ON WATER?

A: WHEN IT'S ICE.

Doodle the hockey player. Is it you?

A: IN THEIR LAUNCH-BOX.

Doodle the box, the rest of the astronaut, and a lunar background.

Q: WHY DID THE PIG HAVE TO SIT ON THE BENCH DURING FOOTBALL PRACTICE?

A: HE PULLED HIS HAMSTRING.

Where's the rest of him? Ham it up!
Doodle a pain-faced piggy!

Q: WHY DO BASKETBALL PLAYERS NEED SO MANY NAPKINS?

A: THEY'RE ALWAYS DRIBBLING.

Finish the unfinished parts of these three players . . . and their food.

# Q: WHY DIDN'T THE CRAB SPEND ANY OF HIS MONEY?

A: BECAUSE HE WAS A PENNY PINCHER.

Draw his twin next to him with a sand dollar.

# About the Author

**Rob Elliott** is the author of *Laugh-Out-Loud Jokes for Kids*, *More Laugh-Out-Loud Jokes for Kids*, *Laugh-Out-Loud Animal Jokes for Kids*, and *Knock-Knock Jokes for Kids* and has been a publishing professional for more than twenty years. Rob lives in **West Michigan**, where in his spare time he enjoys laughing out loud with his wife and five children.

# About the Illustrator

**Jonny Hawkins** is a full-time cartoonist whose work has appeared in over six hundred publications, including *Reader's Digest*, *Parade Magazine*, *The Saturday Evening Post*, and *Guideposts*. His illustrations have appeared in many books including the Chicken Soup for the Soul series, and he has created forty-eight successful page-a-day cartoon calendars (over four hundred thousand sold). He works from his home in **Sherwood, Michigan**, where he lives with his wife, Carissa, and their three children, four cats, and a dog.

# Need More Laughs?

- - - - - - - ✳ - - - - - - -

Visit

## LOLJokesForKids.com

to submit your own joke,
receive FREE printable doodle pages,
and watch the video!

• • •

 *Laugh-Out-Loud Jokes for Kids*

🐦 *@loljokesforkids.com*

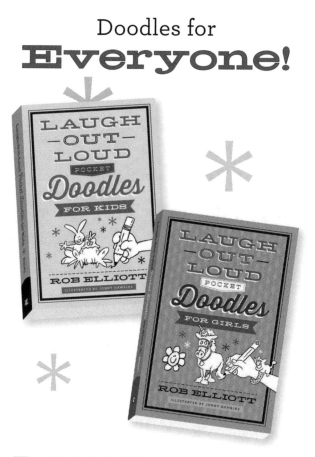